LOVE
IS A
MENTAL
ILLNESS

Folie à Deux

Franco Cardiello

CONTENTS

Section One: Bachelors and Spinsters

Section Two: Lunacy

Section Three: By a Thread

Section Six: Metamorphose

Section Seven: I Must Be Crazy

INTRODUCTION

Psychosis is a mental disorder where a person's thoughts and emotions become detached from reality. Love can carry us into fantasy or drop us into a nightmare. *Love Is a Mental Illness* examines unhealthy behaviors in my toxic relationships.

I endured severe distress from unsafe relationships in my early and mid 20's, and I wrote about it all trying to figure out why my relationships hurt so badly. A decade later, I went through a painful breakup and revisited my past writings about similar situations. Reading my old poems was an emotional trip down memory lane, but I realized how much I've grown since then. So I curated them into this collection.

Each section explores different stages of relationships. These pieces are the outbursts of a confused young man trying to manage his misguided energy, misplaced rage, and unhealthy views of love. I was willing to admit my mistakes and confront my flaws in order to improve. Cathartic writing helps me face complex issues, process trauma, and better understand myself. Raw diary entries allowed me to learn, heal, let go, and move on. Discussing these events helped me break many unhealthy patterns and form new healthy behaviors.

As a silver lining, these relationships encouraged me to study psychology and become a counselor later in life. Although some of the stories are embarrassing, I'm proud to share this collection because it documents the beginning of my self-improvement journey. It illustrates how far I've come as a writer and as a lover.

My journals consist of adult language and themes, including but not limited to sex, abuse, trauma, and death. Perhaps the self-reflection within these stories can help readers gain insights into their own lives. Please make healthy choices and positive changes.

- Franco

If you have any questions or comments, you can DM me on Instagram @Franco_Cardiello or email me at FrancoCardiello@mail.com.

SECTION 1

BACHELORS AND SPINSTERS

Love might be the cure,
but your searching can lead to worse illnesses.

FOLIE À DEUX

Folie à deux is a French term meaning shared madness,
a disorder conceptualized by Charles Lasègue and Jules Falret,
it's a rare mental illness where two people share one delusion –
I think this should be the definition of love

humans yearn for a partner when we're lonely
spending too much time daydreaming of their fantasy
hearts become ecstatic if someone shows them any interest
we barely believe our eyes when we find someone

their similar outlooks make our ideologies seem sensible
this can't merely be some nonsense in our silly minds,
not some hallucination grown out of madness,
How could I be crazy when someone else feels the same way?

So people couple up to avoid loneliness,
isolated dependents induce convictions and demonize outsiders,
many people have gone certifiably mad for a lover
I admit that I've lost my mind on a few occasions

delusion is classified as one person believing something
which the rest of the world widely agrees is untrue
But what if two people believe the same thing?
What if thousands believe?

No true cure exists for darlings sharing this disorder,
partners must separate in order to end a two-sided psychosis,
but even detaching does not guarantee any return to sanity
once alone, we must comfort our lonely hearts again

so romantic bachelors and spinsters restart the process
looking for a new partner to share in their beliefs
because this model of madness is built for two
folie à deux, folie à deux

HABITUAL HEARTS

You remind me of someone I used to love
I'm not sure if that makes me want you more
or fear you more

my exes are all unique inside and out
yet I recognize a shared trait making them fall for me
and that similarity is also what makes me fall for them

engaged by this whatchamacallit
this X factor
this no-word thing

we usually memorize the roads constantly traveled
turns and conditions ingrained in our minds
we could probably drive them blindfolded

but those roads are long gone
we cannot steer our wheels on roads ahead
using old maps that only know the roads in our rearview

if we only experience harmful interactions,
then we may disregard a healthy partner
because we're unsure how to handle alien niceties

we're often drawn to people who feel familiar
even if their behaviors are toxic or dangerous
because we subconsciously follow the same ole patterns

perhaps the definition of insanity
is doing the same thing over and over again
while expecting a new result

so many of us are romantic like that
and foolish like that
human hearts are habitual like that

MAYBE THIS IS CHEATING

My wandering eye
always glances around corners
my selective heart finds many beguiling women
but I'm not cheating on anyone

I'm a single guy looking for a connection
with the potential to fall for any female
staring deep into their seductive eyes
desperate for a sneak peek into my future

maybe I'll get a glimpse of us sharing old age
if I look and listen carefully enough,
maybe I'm searching for something that doesn't exist,
I'm not sure if I believe in fate

I miss my present because I can't live in the now,
always trying to peep into my future
Is it even possible to see that far ahead?
I search for the answers within you

I'm not afraid to bare my soul to a woman
but I fear showing it to the wrong person again
maybe I'm cheating myself
by spying on my future

TEMPORARY COMPANY

Sanity comes and goes
women come and go

people can bring peace into your life
or they can rip it out of you

depression keeps me company most of the time
but that bitch leaves for spells, too

insomnia is an old friend that keeps in touch
but I'm glad we mostly grew apart over the years

you and I are not permanent pieces in each other's lives
but we'll fit good for a limited time

we picked each other because we share a mutual respect
we don't fake a romance or demand commitment

we're the best company we could ask for
but this isn't a future to bet on

we will never regret the time we shared
you and I will remember one another fondly

because we partnered up to fight the madness of sadness
I've said goodbyes and badbyes and all sorts of byes in between

soul mates we were not, forever we won't see
but we were good temporary company in this lonely world

ALL SALES FINAL

Time is one way we try to measure love
because our days are non-refundable

relationships are expensive –
if time is currency

quite a price to pay for our fleeting existence
so I wonder if you and I are wasting our time

my heart wants to invest everything in you
my sexual urges want to empty the bank for you

but I've already squandered a lot of my energy
on women who hurt me and are now long gone

hearts must be spent and shared in this world
but I'm giving pieces of myself to every pretty face

I haven't been frugal
I don't think I'm spending wisely

I ALMOST LOVED YOU

I lose track of time while looking into your eyes,

but I don't lose myself in you, even though I want to.

We share titillating conversations and phenomenal sex,

but I don't miss you when we're apart.

You understand my issues and give me the space I ask for,

but maybe that's why you do not captivate me.

We don't have any grit for traction,

no mountain to climb – no drama to engage.

Something must make people stick or else we slip away.

Dirt and mud are far stickier than cleanliness.

Perhaps your peace is too boring for my traumatized heart.

I find it difficult to settle with you despite your calmness.

Maybe because I think you're too good to be true

and part of me believes that I don't deserve you.

My loneliness almost turned a corner for you,

your sensuality almost had me,

I almost loved you.

OWN WHAT YOU SAY

We must own what we say,
but everyone would hate us
if they heard the words we share in private

just when I connect to someone –
it turns out she's already married,
but she wants to be with me anyway

Can I live with being a homewrecker?
Is her cheating a red flag that I should let fly by?
Did our hearts do anything wrong?

What are we supposed to do with our hearts?
Overwhelmed and swelling for each other,
we can blame love, but we're liable for our actions

Why do these desires consume us both?
I'd think myself mad if you didn't reciprocate,
but we are both filled with madness

you and I come to a fork in the road
I'll happily follow any path so long as you join me
all roads lead to my death if you leave me

we can walk hand-in-hand into a new future
or you could return to your vows
and we'll grow old, occasionally wondering *what if*

he vowed revenge on me
now all three of us stand at this fork in the road
owning what we said

PARADOXICAL

A paradox is a seemingly absurd statement
and a self-contradicting situation
that somehow proves itself to be true
yet doesn't possess a logical reason or solution

you hold me tight until you suddenly drop me
hang all over me for days, then disappear for weeks,
you're the only girl I care about despite my philandering,
we sleep with other people to reassert our freedom

I'm your favorite person, but you like seeing other men
we want us on-call 24/7, but we need plenty of alone time,
we claim to respect each other's space,
but we're only avoiding our fear of commitment

You asked me, *Will we love each other forever?*
We can't see into the future, babe
Are we allowed to take breaks?
Whenever you need, my dear

Who claimed relationships must last forever?
We made no vows, hun
These are fair questions, right?
We're in agreeance, my love

we make love all evening and cuddle all night
until claustrophobia makes us run before brunch
too in love to leave, too afraid to stay
it was too painful to escape our past relationships

mutual friends remind us that we belong together
happy monogamy likely waits for us in the lurch,
but divided hearts polarize our love and fear
two ambivalent hearts ironically devoted

ENTERTAINING SERIOUSNESS

We play in the grey with serious faces
you and I are a good matchup for this game
two talented lovers pushing sexual boundaries

similar sense of humor laughing at dirty jokes
we swap sad stories and cry over comparable sorrow
so two perfect strangers took a chance –

our first date rushed into a week-long trial run
with nowhere to run from our hunting hearts
vacationing in a beach house is a sweet fantasy

quickly intimate and briefly playing house
inquiring minds toying with sex toys
fiddling with futures

I love watching you play with your hair
you hate watching me split hairs in my head
you slip into lingerie in front of the mirror

you pose your most serious proposal
I sit on the edge of the bed
naked, horny, and nervous

you already made up your mind about us
but you're patient with my hesitance
you seriously want us to be together

so I sincerely entertain your idea
we wait for my answer to your question –
Do I love you?

INTO THE DARK

Trust issues limit your communication
I feel the knots in your shoulders
and the cramps in your stomach

I hear your silent cries and non-verbal cues
I see your invisible signs
because I feel the same kind of hurt

I want to take care of that little girl inside you
hoping you can heal the traumatized boy inside me
broken people attract each other that way

your heart shattered and you won't let anyone near it
we built high walls and for good reason
I chip away at mine like a prisoner escaping

you don't want to let me into your mind,
afraid of what I might find,
but I've seen battle and I know about healing

like most people, you barricade your darker side,
but that's the only place I want to go
maybe I'm a fool asking for trouble

but it's hard for damaged people to relax,
let alone around people who never saw war,
oddly pleasant to find someone with similar dark shades

maybe we can help heal our wounds
two empaths are going to see everything clearly
once we head into the dark

SECTION 2

LUNACY

We all love on a spectrum.

POKING HOLES

How much we suffer proves how much we care – right?
We've been miserable for a long time
I thought my patience spoke of my love for you
you thought arguing validated your investment

I guess we were both wrong
because we accomplished very little in our debate,
losing track of mediocre speaking points,
the only thing we learned was how petty we could become

you can express your heart intelligibly to me one day
then you completely shut down the next,
switching between tantrums and silent treatments,
from one extreme to the next along your heart's spectrum

rage tore through me when I hit my wit's end
until I cried because I ran out of words to scream,
you couldn't comprehend what I was trying to say,
our words slide from meaningless to earth shattering

I tried to poke well-intentioned holes in your argument
simply to let new ideas shine in,
you merely punctured my character out of anger
misconstruing our conversation for a war

fears and concerns should be met with support
instead, we attack each other
I punch holes in your logic while you stab holes in my ego,
riddled with wounds – we bleed out

FUCK YOU, BABY

My erections for you are just as hard as our issues
I yearn for your body, but rail against your ignorance
our arguments trigger my regrettable rage
yet I touch myself while I write this

you're wet during our screaming matches
I'm erect while you curse me out in your lingerie
I'd never put my hands on you
but we need to unleash our frustrations

so we cry while we kiss and then we fuck it out of us
I pound on you – just the way you like
then you ride me until you release all your energy
we broke our headboard and keep breaking our hearts

shattered glass scars your hand and ankle
your digging nails rip open my back and arms
painting each other with bruises and bite marks
while the museless gawk at art

our fights are not average
put the knife down
our sex is not average
I said put it down

our hearts are dysfunctional delinquents
I hate how much I love you
because I love you as much as I hate you
and that's an impossible love

CALL OF THE WILD

Dating an adrenaline junky
racing sports cars
sometimes they were stolen
pushing the limits of mortality

anarchist raging against authority
thrill seeking through petty larceny
I recognized the fury in her eyes
the same fierce look I once had

I quit committing crimes and I buried immature desires
people don't see what's boiling beneath my surfacethese days
but she saw through my new lifestyle
and she summoned my old hibernating urges

she experimented with drugs
while I was early in my sobriety
she wanted sex in public
while this felon played it safe

she's unruly and becomes unhinged when bored
while I became disciplined to earn my counseling license
she was my last taste of freedom
before I transitioned into a responsible office job

her disorder engaged my pragmatic brain
yet she bypassed my critical thinking
by stroking my ego with her cocksure mouth
and bringing adventure back to my boring life

but I had to escape her dangerous world
so I begged her to join me before she hurt herself
and I showed her a peaceful living as an alternative
but she'd rather stay in the wild

LOVING TO SURVIVE

Hostages develop bonds with their captors
when spending intimate time together during captivity.
Detainees may become physically attracted to abductors.
This condition is called Stockholm syndrome.

They refuse to cooperate with police or authorities
because they believe in the humanity of their captor.
Victims might agree with a criminal's reasoning
even if they wouldn't act in the same manner.

"Identifying" is a self-defense mechanism to help one cope
- kidnappings, internment camps, and human trafficking
- victims defend partners amid domestic violence
- children mimic the behaviors of abusive parents

A woman held me prisoner through trauma bonding.
Nothing to do but get to know her and fall in love.
She told me her life story so I'd empathize with her suffering.
I hated the people who hurt her, so we shared enemies.

Controls and bonds both make people stick around,
but one way to tell the difference between them
is that a control won't allow you to leave when you try,
and a bond feels sad when you leave, yet still wishes you well.

We did what we needed to in order to survive.
She lied, accused, blamed, and manipulated.
I'm free from her and her heinous crimes now
yet I still don't wish any punishment on her.

SEEKING ASYLUM

We had sex everywhere all the time
because we couldn't control our fervor

horny enough to fuck in a hospital bathroom
and behind large nightclub speakers

but there's a flip side to that passion
heated arguments drove her to violence

I couldn't keep my hands off her curves
she couldn't keep her hands to herself when angry

she clawed at my face in fights
because she couldn't win with words

she sunk her teeth and nails into me
because she couldn't climax until I bled

spoke in her baby voice and gave me a blow job
instead of apologizing with mature articulation

doctors evaluated me in the psychiatric ward
she is by far the craziest person I ever dated

but I must be crazy, too
because I still love her

PADDING

I check-in this madhouse
no room with a view
because padded walls don't have windows
we all need some padding in this hard world

they took my shoelaces
and gave me pills I couldn't pronounce
I took their surveys
they gave me a mental status exam

the doctor is in
but I'm afraid even the doctor is in on this
maybe this is all a conspiracy
the voice in my head doesn't trust anyone

they lend me a miniature pencil
and supervise me while I write
my thoughts are all about her
pages and pages all dedicated to her

INKBLOTS

Psychiatrist Hermann Rorschach created a test
for clients to look at abstract symmetrical inkblots
and report what they see in the images

so therapists analyze their patients' perception
and interpretations may identify mental disorders

there are some common answers
but people see different objects in the images
and love is just as abstract as an inkblot

What did I see in you?
What did you see in me?

I see myself in you
because significant others
are often our mirror image

the things I hate about you
merely reflect what I hate in me

your face is perfectly symmetrical
but your head is full of monsters
and I can't quit staring at you

I analyze abstract inkblots
but all I see is you

I WAS SANE ONCE

Sanity intact with stability and peace
rationale guided my safe decisions
until you stormed into my life

you claim that withholding isn't technically lying
petty lies while charging me with false accusations
your projections are like a drive-in movie screen

you're a gaslighter questioning my every move
purposely undermining everything I say
changing the topic and refusing to apologize

you hang guilt trips over me
blame me for your questionable behavior
and refuse to take onus of your actions

emasculating my ego only intensifies my masculinity
my rage for you spills over onto hurting other men
I don't even remember how that gun got in my hand

my family begged me to leave you
now it's difficult to remember my life before we met
but I swear I was sane once

EVERY COLOR

Your aura projects every color of the rainbow
sliding up and down your polarizing highs and lows
plot grandiose ideas and spend money you don't have
and sporadically have sex with strangers

your rationale flies out the window
while your inhibitions plummet
you write poems in gibberish
on binges of drugs and alcohol to level yourself off

a week without sleep leads to a severe head-on collision
you can't escape your bed, trapped under blankets
as if caught in the rubble of a demolished building,
but I promise your world did not collapse

we fear your highs as much as your lows
and we hear your sincere remorse,
but we don't want your apologies
we just want you to take your medication again

I'm sorry I couldn't keep up with your manic energy
or comfort your pains well enough when you crashed,
but I was a fool to think that I had any say in the matter
and I'm exhausted from trying to stabilize you

euphoria in your foreground, sorrow in your background,
I waited for your stable middle ground before breaking up
I informed your family and doctor – they're ready to support you
but I must leave you now for my own wellbeing

your aura encapsulates every color that nature has to offer,
but you no longer see the forest for the trees
I zoom out to envision the bigger picture
I walk away in tears as your rainbow shines over us

I STILL SEE ORANGE

Staring into the sun too long
will burn our retinas
we still see orange after closing our eyes
until it softens back to black

I must look away from you now
because you're stalking my social media
and searching my computer,
harassing women you're suspicious of

you're throwing tantrums in public
I can't subject myself to this kind of behavior
so I break up with you,
but you can't accept it

you can't stop crying and you call out of work,
scratch at your wrists and threaten to kill yourself,
you can tell me anything,
but not a guilt trip

don't threaten self-harm if you think it will make me stay,
don't try to keep me through extortion,
I can't leave knowing you might keep your deadly promise,
please seek professional help

I've seen you cut your wrists on your lowest days,
but this is the first time you've swallowed a fist full of pills
I left in tears and we haven't spoken in months
I close my eyes to rest, but I still see orange

SECTION 3

BY A THREAD

Lost people tend to find other people who are lost.
And that makes them feel more found.
But they're just two people lost together.

THE WAY WE MOVE

Our actions impact each other, often unwittingly,
individuals start new behaviors after becoming a couple
so I've been paying attention to the way we move

how you and I dance around each other
I'll never be able to scale, track or duplicate your rhythm
like emptying a bag of marbles onto a hardwood floor

but I do catch some patterns in our interactions
these familiar traits remind me of my parents
and that scares the hell out of me

you mustn't try to pin me down
I need ample space to roam
we all have our limits and boundaries

some people believe cheating is unforgivable
while some couples enjoy open-relationships
so we must agree on a set of rules

some people are free to run wild
while others feel trapped
so we must compromise some of our motions

chasing kids and careers
our busy worlds spin so fast
no wonder you and I are dizzy

we need to pause to get in sync
relearn each other's moves
I want us to understand how we sway

Who knows where our ways will lead us?

HOW TO BEND A TREE

We didn't stop loving each other
but our needs have changed
couples struggle to remain in sync

our transformations sometimes correlate
but they're seldom in tandem
change is good, but requires friction and tension

I truly want the best for you
How do we support each other's growth
if we know we're branching in different directions?

I want to share this journey of our ever-changing lives
but perceptions alter and desires waver
How do two people keep moving in the same direction?

Hoping our spouse's leash offers enough slack
we try to decide on some paths to take together
but commitments are difficult to maintain

big stubborn trees are strong and immovable
until bad enough weather uproots them
while flexible palm trees bend to survive the storm

tree shaping is the art of training trees
controlling the direction of branches
I believe you and I should study arbor sculpture

maybe we can retrain and guide new patterns
people design beautiful tree art all over the world
I don't see why we can't do the same for ourselves

LOOSE ENDS

Struggling to string our thoughts like threading a needle
sewing the fabric of our lives comes with occasional pricks
you and I weave our intricate patterns
and knit our intimate futures together

the slightest flaws easily trigger your compulsion
like a loose strand hanging from a favorite old sweater
comfortable with sentimental value
but we're damaged from years of wear and tear

sometimes we need to leave well enough alone
but you lack self-control, my dear
fixating on your fear of loose ends
looking too closely and obsessing over perfection

trying to measure your split ends in the mirror
precisely cut, trim, and alter every detailed angle
broken strands entangle despite relentless combing
please be grateful for beautiful hair and comfortable sweaters

you yanked on the tiniest of strands
we unraveled amid your complex neurosis
and you unwittingly pulled us apart
now we're hanging on by a thread

ONCE DECLARED

You said you loved me once
I declared my love, too

we circle each other like hands on clocks
all day I love you

beginnings and endings are only a moment apart
like numbers 1 and 12 on a clock

we sit on far ends of our couch like 9 and 3
but I want you next to me all the time

I desperately want to shake this monotony
revisit the spontaneity we used to live in

drop inhibitions and grab the passion we once coveted
we carelessly let time pass by as if we could get it back

I still miss you when you go out
I wonder if you still miss me when I'm gone

we don't pay each other too much mind these days
but I never once stopped loving you

maybe we grew too comfortable on our bed of roses
ignored the thorns amid the heady scent

considering all the wild times we shared
all the dreams we discussed and plans we made

you said you loved me once
I declared my love, too

BY THE WAYSIDE

We vowed our alliance once – us against the world

but now all we do is fight each other

Don't you see that I'd start another world war for us?

I guess you'd rather fight your internal battle alone

I'm still your ally, but you choose to wave me off

to die on the frontlines of a war in the back of your mind

though I'm not sure if you have any fight left in you

I feel you detaching from me as you fade into the unknown

I used to lose myself in you and you would lose yourself in me

now we're both lost in the middle of nowhere

you've given up on just about everything

and I fear you might have given up on yourself

– that's what worries me the most

Where did your fight go? When did you lose it?

You always hunted knowledge, adventure, and pleasure

you had such zest for life and wanted to share it with me

until your commitment to us fell by the wayside

TOGETHER ALONE

Our dog rests on the couch and the fish ignores us
you sit on the opposite side of the room
I feel a great distance despite our close proximity
living worlds apart within the same apartment
together alone, together alone

side by side in silence at our his and hers sink
we avoid brushing each other in our hallway
like commuters passing on the train
like strangers coexisting in a public restroom
When did we become cellmates?

There was a time when we cherished our time
we loved each other immensely once
and we held hands everywhere
our dissonant hearts used to adore one another
but we lost our winks and forgot how to play grab-ass

now you sleep on our couch
while I wait for you in bed at night
we shared blankets and pillows for years
but we stopped sharing sex
maybe we never shared a dream

you eat meals standing up in the kitchen
refusing to join me at our table
sharing this 860-square foot apartment
you might as well be halfway around the globe
together alone, together alone

THE ABYSS BETWEEN US

I overlook the empty chair at our table
where laughter used to join us
before it died and left us like vilomahs

you assume I don't hear you crying over the kitchen sink
because I stay on the other side of our house
and refrain from comforting you
remembering when I watched my mother as a boy
sobbing while she washed our dinner plates

I wanted to kill the world that hurt her
but I was just a little boy then
I didn't have any idea what to do
now I watch you cry in a similar fashion
and as a man I still don't know what to do

you are two very different women
crying for very different reasons
but I'm the same man feeling like the same boy
in the same predicament – at the same loss
and I want to kill the world for you

I found you crying on the kitchen floor
you told me that you were poison
you refused to say anything else to me
and refused to speak with a professional

slip into a dark hole where no one can reach you
I follow you where no one can reach either of us
love is big enough to swallow the entire universe
so we descend into the abyss between us

CHASING HORIZONS

Driving through our own private Idaho
we sit in silence on our shared road trip
but we're pursuing different horizons

entire day of driving through nothing but fields
you're not the same girl you were yesterday
afraid of everything outside your window

we're a dying couple visiting lively cities
built in the middle of nowhere
no real business being there

you sat in my passenger seat for three years
dropped into my life
with no real business being there

fly down highways and creep through side streets
weave in and out of bustling cities and ghost towns
crisscrossing the Bible Belt and the Rust Belt

without ever asking borders for permission
just like the way we test each other's limits
and learn our own ambits along the journey

two passengers sharing a ride
yet headed in two different directions
grinding on the rims of our equanimity

cities take on a life of their own
we built a life of our own on the fringes
far too close to the edge of the world

massive Midwest clouds so close to earth
we're expecting the sky to crash on us
before we drive off the cliff chasing our horizon

SAID INSTEAD

I scream, *Leave me alone*
instead of asking for help
with my taxing career
and traumatic past

you claim I don't do enough for you
instead of explaining what you need
so we stew as if we're alone
instead of communicating clearly

we're not mind readers
yet you hate if I put words in your mouth
and when I can't guess your feelings
but your silent treatments speak in volumes

I avoid you for a few days
instead of explaining that you hurt me
I pray for an inkling of telepathy
because I want you to understand me, too

you scream, *I don't want this anymore*
instead of being thankful for what we have
I remember the beautiful things I want to say
and I regret all the ugly shit I said instead

LAST LEG

You're not right in the head
I'm not right in the heart

neither of us is right about our argument
but we're right in each other's faces

screaming matches squeeze the life out of us
and painful cries strangle us

we pull out our tools to "fix" one another
fine line between surgery and butchering

determined to make this work
but we're getting nowhere

two people sharing one delusion
pushing the limits of our sanity

happiness awaits us
across this river of ego

we might have burned our bridges
but perhaps we find a ferry of compromise

heart on my sleeve, beaten and tattered
all my cards on the table, bent and scattered

after everything we've been through –
I don't know how we're still standing

ZENITH

We were strangers
yet fell madly in love instantly
enamored without suspicion of infatuation

but we met our vertex
I grip the edges
but you'll soon let go of loving me

little
by little
by little

sure, my gestures act like speed bumps
slowing you down while you slide away from me
reminding you of our once climbing affection

but you ran out of gusto when you met our zenith
our great highs are all downhill from here
your admiration for me will fall fast and stop abruptly

a few fights and make-ups momentarily confuse us
it won't feel like it happened gradually over time
until nothing but an old photo of us is left as proof

we'll think of each other on the regular
until our thoughts decrease
weekly – monthly – yearly

our tiny hearts inflated for each other
now they're sadly deflating
little

by little
by
little

LOUD SILENCE

Sitting in your father's old station wagon
we haven't spoken in thirty minutes
rain bangs as if trying to break in
water sneaks through the leaking sunroof

each drop slides through the cracks
and lands on us like your tears
we let each other in
but we can't let tears back in

we struggle to breathe,
but not from great sex in the backseat,
seems like only yesterday
we were teenagers panting into bliss back there

now we're short of breath from hard crying
we put too many miles on us
like your station wagon's odometer
this old car will eventually break down, too

I'm not afraid of getting wet
but I don't want to leave you
you're not kicking me out
because you don't want me to leave either

haven't glanced at each other in thirty minutes
we don't know what to do with all this
our hearts deduce nothing
we sit quietly and watch the loud rain

LAST NIGHT OF LOVE

Perhaps this will be our last night of love
before my days begin to forget her

she and I used to stay awake for all-nighters
sharing endless dreams under countless stars

but every sunrise brings night to its end
I no longer feel her, so I feel I've lost her

I don't see a single star in my sky tonight
not a slight glimmer of hope for us

a cold and lonely pillow rests next to mine
no longer a warm indentation of her

we may spend more days trying to forget someone
than the number of days we shared with them

nobody can predict our final goodbyes
we can't foresee what our last words to someone will be

Do you remember the last time you talked to your ex?
Do you recall the last thing you said to them?

I begged her, *Please, just leave me alone*
those were my last words to her

I don't remember the exact day we fell in love
nor am I certain which day we fell out of love

but I remember the last night we made love
but it's difficult for me to identify our last night of love

SECTION 4

PSYCHOSOMATIC

Your heart is in constant chaos.
You have to train your brain
to be an effective crisis intervention worker.

JAGGED US

I see all the damage lingering in your eyes
aftereffects of the torture they put you through

you and I don't trust this sharp world
filled with people who ripped at our hearts

leaving ours forever serrated
but you and I are soft on each other

my heart bleeds for the Lennie's of the world
petting soft things too hard
huge hearts, simple brains, and a big dream

you and I treat each other with good intentions
despite our rough edges cutting one other

we're comfortable in our broken spaces
because we're used to it

something about us feels like home
even if it's a broken home

we tried pulling away from each other
but we only created a tighter hold
like a Chinese finger trap

your tremble is merely an impulse
the aftershock from previous earthquakes

our sawtoothed addictions won't let go
we scrape each other the more we try to slither away

nothing evens out in this uneven world
so we rip each other with our jagged hearts

SILENT CALLS

She watches me with tears in her eyes
through my desktop computer's video chat
but I can't look at her
so I write in my notebook
my head rests sideways on my left arm
escapism through literature

though it's mostly doodles
I have no words for my paper
or for her
we ran out of old words
as we stumbled upon new emotions
after she told me the news

she told me she loved me
she never meant to hurt me
she knew she had herpes
she watches a man silently disappear
regressing to childhood
while the buried boy emerges

traumas resurrect and resurface
my mind tries to fend them off
this is not good for either of us
I can't bring myself to hang up
she stays online just to watch me
even though we have nothing left to say

maybe loneliness is better when shared
so I stay on video without looking
and on these calls without talking
this has become our latest routine
she watches and cries while I doodle and suppress
keep answering our silent calls

UNBURN

Heavy curtains seal my dark hotel room
but a warm sunbeam sneaks underneath the drapes
bright orange strikes across the floor like a match

I know how cold and dark this world is
especially after the way you left me
fuming alone with a bottle of Jack Dan's

I want to burn this building down
dying embers desperate for your heat
like melting candle wax on your chest and thighs

it's too late for us now to rekindle anything
whiskey and cigarettes burn a hole in my chest
where my heart used to be

you're the cancer in my exhale
and the regrets in my ashtray
as I sift through our irreversible ashes

but it's impossible to unburn
so I'm here smoldering alone
under this hotel room's NO SMOKING sign

SKYSCRAPERS

Your insecurities are merely illusions
just like buildings can't scrape the sky
a sweet girl believing bitter lies of self-doubt
your big heart carries little confidence

I held you up as high as I could
you thought you were flying
but my adoration for you was no match
for your insistent cynicism

maybe I held you up higher than I should have
giving your petrified heart vertigo
and as soon as I needed a break
you blamed your crash-landing on me

but I cannot prop you up all the time
you must take onus of your actions
you were diffident and timid your entire life
yet now you blame your uncertainties on me

I'll hold your hand when you're ready to face your fears
but I won't let you accuse me of creating them
some of your concerns are valid
but your tantrums are brutal and merciless

so I kiss your thick forehead one last time
before I leave you and this toxic city
and we break each other's hearts
underneath these skyscrapers

EXPOSURE THERAPY

Clueless to the outside world
the girl in a plastic bubble
sheltered and afraid of everything
escaped her overbearing religious mother

full of questions and full of nerves
you asked me for help, so I said,
Hold on, this is going to hurt
(both of us)

I held up a brutally honest mirror
to highlight your worst flaws
you hated me for inching you toward your fears
but I held your hand as we progressed

I empowered you to stand up for yourself
and taught you self-defense moves
I taught you how to drive a car and how to move in bed
how to invest in stocks and how to move in the street

you grew an unhealthy attachment to me
and you relied on me for everything
but you need a professional – not a boyfriend
I don't want a teacher-student relationship

I can't be your therapist, lover, teacher, and father
this doctor-patient dynamic confuses our sex life
you should be desensitized to your fears by now
you must learn to navigate on your own

our relationship exposed my shortcomings as well
so it's time I leave you and start working on myself again

DRAINED

Can you see us behind the mountain?
Can you envision our future through the clouds?

Can you squeeze through the horizon?
Can you swim through your overflowing doubts?

You left because you couldn't see a future
I tried convincing you, but I'm not very persuasive

I don't feel alone yet
maybe you haven't been gone long enough

alone in the shower, flooding in tears
drowning in a sea of thoughts

where I used to wash your hair
and hold you until we ran out of hot water

memories rain on me
a bottle of your fancy conditioner sits on my shelf

doing nothing like unspoken apologies
useless like broken promises

I can't stop visualizing our potential
seeing everything we could have had

water running like my mind
I wish to be still with you

JUNKYARD

You called me junk because I was broken
(you heard no argument from me)

but I hope you realize you're as broken as I am
and you're headed to the same burial grounds

where the discarded wedding rings are melted down
a final resting place where inside jokes go to die

and spirits quit counting anniversaries
after they live hard, love hard, drink hard, die hard

mountains of miscellaneous memories
piles of dysfunctional hearts and mounds of secret affairs

corroded debris laying on top of each other on the ground
like desperate hearts in a stranger's bed

this man is merely a pile of junk
sitting on a collection of rusted regrets

OUR BED IS A GRAVEYARD

We had to have it at least a few times per day
in a park in daylight, a back row of a movie theater
and a train ride from the city into the countryside
we lived for the fuck of each other

we couldn't keep our hands to ourselves
we used to cuddle for hours
now we don't even hold hands
we don't share time or a gaze

we're both very sexual people
yet we haven't touched in days
we haven't kissed in weeks
I don't think you've loved me in months

I don't recall the last time we had sex
the last time we laughed together
the last time I played with your hair
I swear we used to enjoy our company

Do you remember how we used to be?
I'm not writing about our lack of orgasms
I'm concerned with the underlying issues
that drives a wedge between us

I still want to kiss you every morning
make love to you all day long
and cuddle with you in the evening
but I doubt I ever cross your mind

your heart stopped beating for me
so we lay lifeless side by side
like dead strangers buried next to each other
in adjacent cemetery plots

ALTERNATIVE

Winds have to start and end somewhere
but those markers remain unfound
births and deaths unrecorded

I know the precise moment I fell in love with you
the only people in a dark restaurant late at night
your face glowing in the candle on the table

I knew at that very moment I lost all control
I accepted the fact that you owned me
and I surrendered before we ordered

I also remember the day we died
the first time I raised my voice at you
and I drove away from you in a parking lot

you were the family I never had
also the future I never deserved
I refuse to go back to where I came from

only a few certainties in this uncertain world
I'm sure I no longer love you
and I'm sure I'll always love you

you never know when or where
but surely invisible breezes will tickle you again
graze your skin and make the hair stand on your neck

I remember our births and deaths
I redirect my agony into poetry for you
because the alternative –

well, you don't want to know

SECTION 5

SEQUELAE

The more you ignore your issues,
the more they harm the people around you.

WHERE WE WENT WRONG

Clair de Lune plays on repeat
Maker's Mark on two rocks
desperate for an answer
wondering where she and I went wrong

I prayed, meditated, and spoke to clueless therapists
talked to friends and punched holes in walls
hit the bottle alone and drank with slutty barflies
but nothing in this stanza holds the answers I seek

a homeless guy suggested I should eat and shower
a prostitute reminded me to masturbate
an insomniac advised me to get some sleep
a therapist didn't say much at all

not meant to be – what a lazy generic excuse
she can't give me a clear answer though
I tried everything to distract myself
but I can't stop wondering where we went wrong

WEARY OBSESSIONS

I haven't showered in a few days
listening to morose music
and watching sad movies
I don't cook or clean or go outside
I haven't vacuumed or dusted

you'd be shocked to see my laundry pile
my kitchen sink overflowing
or the crumbs on my table
my OCD took a vacation from nagging
allowing me to sulk like a pig in shit

compulsions stopped pestering me
but they're staring at me in disbelief and disgust
people have exasperated my obsessions
but nobody ever deactivated them before
that's the power you have over me

fixated on counting, organizing, and cleaning
now these lifelong tics are lifeless, as am I
couch potatoes with eyes only for you
tics will slowly but surely return
but I'm not sure if you will

TAME ME IN BED

You tried to tame me to one side of the bed
but even though we were wild together –
my limbs still strayed off our mattress
leaving you behind to wait for my return

until you decided to not wait any longer
now I stare at your stains on my sheets
and spread naked on my bed without you
envisioning your body joining me

my bedroom has been empty for months
but I still see your outline in my bed
I cuddle with my pillows and visions of you
I must learn to sleep without you

you haven't slept next to me in so long
but memories of you still nuzzle through the night
I'm not sure how long your visitant spirit will keep this up
because you're sleeping with another man these days

the guy I know you don't care for
let alone as deeply as you cared for me
perhaps my apparition slides into his bed
splitting your heart, dividing you and him

tossing alone in the middle of my huge mattress
with plenty of unoccupied space to roam
so tie my wrists to the bedposts if you must
just return to our bedroom and tame me to our bed

BLURRY BEAUTY

We saw each other for who we truly were
but I remember your final look at me

and I understand why you had to leave me
so my teary eyes leave everything blurry

so many beauties want me to admire them
hanging around my peripherals

but my vision can't focus on any of them
all those women smear into each other

you and I looked just right
but my cheating smudged everything

trying to find you again through my smeared morals
I dream of the day I can clear things up

and I know I have to earn that privilege
though you don't even want to look at me right now

flashes of you spark in my dark mind
like fireflies at night

lost in my foggy mind
seeing you in bokeh

PICTURESQUE

Photographers take perfect pictures of sundaes,
zestful puppies want to cuddle,
babies laugh when you tickle them

life only has a few moments still untouched,
your face was as perfect as a sundae photo,
happy as a puppy, adorable as a baby

you were perfect to me
I was perfect for you
[that's how we framed it]

our world view was straight enough,
but sure enough we screwed it up
I guess lovers do that

from our fights and sex
to black eyes and forgiveness
nothing left but lies and empty apologies

the whole thing was a mess
and neither of us knew how to clean it up
so we just walked away from it all

with blood on our hands
we left our remains on the ground
everything eventually gets adulterated

just know that I'll always remember you
as one of life's pure moments
before we messed it all up

BUT YOU'RE NOT HERE

There's nothing I can do at night
to stop thinking about you
I play jazz and sit in the dark
I write a few despondent words in your honor

sometimes I jerk off on desperate days
a few tears escape on dark evenings
strange girls keep me company on lonely nights
mostly I just pace in circles and scribble my chicken scratch

I don't fiend for bottles or fluster over cheap thrills
but I've polished plenty of smooth whiskeys and asses
some odd women try to even me out
and crooked girls try to straighten me out

I haven't thrown a temper tantrum since I was a child
but I put my fist through a wall the other day
just for old times' sake, I guess
traumatic memories saw an opening to return

like an old girlfriend popping up out of nowhere
because she hasn't fully let go of me yet
so I either have to hit the decline button
or we have to screw one last time for closure

vices are thieves lurking in shadows
waiting to attack when I'm alone
robbing me of everything
but they won't take my sadness away

I don't have a good excuse for my lonely behavior
What else am I supposed to do?
I tried everything to stop thinking of you
you can't judge me though
because you're not here

NONE OF THEM ARE YOU

Desperate to replace you
I recruit more women to join my crass plan
yet I feel more alone with each passing day

I've crawled between countless sheets
and I lost track of the thread count
no matter how many girls fall in my bed –

none of these women feel like home

we trade philosophies and swap witty banter
but just because we exchange seduction
doesn't mean we share anything at all

I grabbed hundreds of waists, slept on dozens of breasts,
chased a thousand asses, and hid between countless thighs
I lose myself in their bodies because I can't find you

none of these women feel like you

moaning competitions to win my affection
kinky girls entice me with dirty promises
sweet women try to bribe me with commitment

but these girls are merely half-ass versions of you
I've looked closely, but they resemble no comparison
they could never replace a fraction of you

none of them are you

HER ABSENCE

I try to focus on what's in front of me
but I feel the empty space next to me

she always lounged in bed while I scribbled notes
until she got bored and threw a pillow at me

as if I could ever forget she was by my side
so I'd jump in bed and wrap her up

she'd laugh like a giddy little girl
her smile brightened my entire day

she cherished my goofy faces and cartoon voices
because I'm quite serious most of the time

she basked in the realization
that she was the cause for my seldom giddiness

I usually didn't want to bother her with the details
but sometimes she would read my writing

even if she didn't fully understand poetry
that wasn't the point, let alone a necessity

but I guess I didn't play with her enough
and she couldn't get serious enough

cuddling our days away seems like a lifetime ago
I try to focus, but it's impossible to ignore her absence

the empty space next to me she once filled
like the hollow space in my heart that she still owns

FINE SUSPENDED PARTICLES

Particle memories of us float around my head
and linger amid the places we shared beauty

we slept in a tent under a west coast sky in the desert
it's almost impossible to remove sand once you track it in

we made love in a northeast lake one summer evening
memories of that lake mist me like drizzling rain

specks of dust blanket our old photo album now
chakras congested with regret and confusion

you were my world and I was yours
spotty memories like stars in our distance

but all stars eventually burn into a black hole
leaving dense remnants behind

my fine suspended particle memories of us
float around me to obscure my atmosphere

FRAGMENTS

You loiter in my heart long after you left
not like perfume on my sheets
more like resin in my pipe

your residue sticks to me
thoughts of you linger
like the stench of cigarette smoke

broken memories scattered everywhere
I'm trying to fill in the blanks
while splinters of time stab me all over

it's not serious enough to shed blood
but the pain is in the unwelcomed focus it requires
to pinpoint the fine slivers and pluck them out of me

remembering the torture I endured
like shards of glass from a shattered wine bottle
since I quit getting high and drunk with you

stoned and in love
now I'm sober
solemn as a grave

recollecting fragments of us

LIVING WITHOUT

I never had a desire for luxuries
never a need for materialistic things

I've gone days without food
a poor kid is accustomed to living without

but I don't know if I can live without you

I lost you, so now I lose myself in other women
unable to find what I need within them

unable to find myself inside them
because I already know who I am

but I don't feel like myself without you

the most comfortable bed feels like a park bench
when you're not sleeping by my side

some people say I don't deserve you
and they're right

but I never gave a shit about anyone's opinion

you were my backbone
nothing but a slouch if you don't balance me

I wasn't much before, but I'm less of a man without you
I was a different person when we were together

my heart hopes that man sees the light of day again

SECTION 6

METAMORPHOSE

You cannot "fix" people,
but you can start relationships
where everyone involved
has a chance for personal growth.

GRAVE IN ME

I stand over this pit
mourning my own grave,
the hole you dug in my heart,
the chasm you left when you left

loneliness digs into me
carving through my chest,
whittling away at my ribs,
emptiness deepening inside of me

I'm desperately trying to fill this hole
force feeding myself booze and orgasms,
anything that might help me feel good,
but nothing revives me

I realized you weren't the gravedigger at all
this empty space was ripped open years prior,
but you sat in this puddle with me,
your leaving enabled me to feel the breeze in this valley

you cradled me like a baby until you left
so I wouldn't notice my hole as much,
now I'm alone again in the depths of my despair,
and my grave cradles me like a stillborn

I realize I was only burying you with me
and for that I apologize to you,
nothing can fill this hole inside me,
but the love of a woman is the closest fit

alone, I tiptoe around tiny graves
until another woman buries me alive

INSTANT REPLAY

I'm glad I kept your voicemails
I replayed your messages a few dozen times
because I enjoyed hearing your happy voice
but these recordings are also sad reminders

I wanted to celebrate your successes
but this dark filter wrapped around me
is as real as the air we breathe
even though we can't touch it

I couldn't touch your happiness
and you were incapable of feeling my sadness
your occasional sweetness and constant beauty
are in stark contrast to your ugliest qualities

I used to listen to your recordings
because I missed your voice
now I listen as a reminder –
your little voice highlights our biggest differences

MY BEST

I walked away from your unhealthy definitions of love,
but I still miss you at times

I think about us starting over
because I remember all the good times,

but I realize now that I don't miss *you*,
instead, I miss the good moments *I* created

so I threw out all the junk we've accumulated,
oversized teddy bears, and arts and crafts,

all the meaningless gifts collecting dust,
toothbrush, pajamas, and all your crap left behind

I threw out mementos to remove reminders,
but I could never erase visions of your face

I don't want to forget you entirely,
so I kept our photos

I don't regret giving you my best though,
not too many people can say they gave theirs

I'm proud of my efforts despite our separation
and I still wish you my best

SMALL TALK IN VENICE

A gentle woman placed her hand on my wounds,
caring for this broken man in her tender way

leisurely strolls through a sleepy beach town
          during a west coast spring,
though I didn't live in this neighborhood

sitting in the sand, admiring a sunset;
a fantasy day for her escapism
          was melancholy for me

it's odd how small talk to one person
might be perceived as love letters by another

we shared an aimless search for happiness,
two lonely people in need of company

yet even amid the perfect ambiance –
we still inhabited an atmosphere that felt all wrong

sometimes I'd forget she was by my side
when we went on our long silent hikes

(lost in my thoughts, memories, fears, and torment)

she said she loved me, but I never said it back,
three little words come with heavy clauses

I didn't want to talk about anything at all,
she asked me questions so I wouldn't be silent,
she felt enamored as I forced small talk

STILL PROCESSING

Past lovers linger in my heart like smoke
wild women pursued me with fire in their eyes

they truly believed relationships were war
always needing to fuck, fight, fuck, fight, repeat

some airy girls breezed through my life with ease
like water without taste – leaving no ripples in their wake

I'm grateful, but it's easy to forget bland memories
compared to the lionesses who ravaged me

details of long-gone women continue to fade
while other recollections of girls become distorted

and a few nightmares remain clear as day
as miscellaneous remnants of my love life amalgamate

desperate to catch the patterns
hoping to learn the lessons as fast as possible

a goddess could enter my life with the best intentions
but can still unwittingly wake up my hibernating fears

no woman can currently reach me
until I resolve everything that's happened thus far

I'm still processing
...

ONE WEEK OF COMMISERATING

Have you ever consoled someone who's grieving?
A bond develops quickly and grows deep roots,
intense emotions entangle amid the rush,
and bombarded hearts misconstrue the situation.

You happily escaped your life to care for me for a week
while I moped in pain away from the woman I loved.
You gladly explored a new city and my personal depths.
You kept me company in bed, in the shower, and in spirit.

You made love to my body like a porn star.
Caressed my heart like a tender mother.
You helped me the best you knew how.
I truly appreciate your caregiving.

Your nurturing ways gravitated to my suffering.
You took on the caregiver role and tended to my injuries.
My hibernation was ironically your vacation.
My dormant state ran concurrently with your fantasy.

I'm hurting, but I'm strong enough to go on alone.
You acted surprised when I said we must go our own ways,
even though you knew our time was temporary,
yet believed this commiserating would last forever.

You helped me sweep up my broken pieces,
but you wanted more from me than I was able to return
without realizing that I wasn't nearly ready for you,
underestimating the true severity of my injuries.

I'll continue to heal without a nurse
and you'll wait for your next patient.
A caregiver doesn't know what to do with herself
if she doesn't have a broken man to nurture.

CAN'T GET IT UP

You're an imaginative lady full of unfulfilled fantasies
with many cheerless years of neglect and pent-up desires.
I explained how I couldn't fall in love with anyone
because a woman already consumed me.

You persuaded me against my better judgment
even though my heart wasn't ready,
you struggled to understand my mental block,
so I write this to help you step into my shoes and into my heart.

Despite my caveat, you loved me anyway,
and screwed my brains out,
but orgasms can't erase my past
and lingerie won't heal my wounds.

None of that dopamine you summoned
could ever trick my despondent heart.
You laid quite a fairytale on my doorstep
and asked me to love you as if I have a choice.

I asked my heart for an answer while you waited for a verdict.
I warned you how the odds were stacked against you
so it would be wildly selfish of me to ask you to wait.
My broken heart cannot in good conscience ask you to.

I sincerely ask you to walk away from my debris.
I swear you did nothing wrong throughout our interactions.
I'm too injured right now, wounds too raw.
This is all happening too fast, too much, too soon.

You want me to love you, but I just can't do it right now
like when a naked woman is ready to make love,
but an exhausted man can't get it up for her.
I swear I tried for you, but my heart isn't working.

OUT OF HEART

I sat with my thoughts in silence,
stewing while my ingredients broke down,
but she sat next to me the entire time,
sharing coffee and meals and smiles.

She told herself, *this is peaceful,*
the writer needs to think,
and I'm glad he invited me here
to enjoy the shared silence while he works.

Though that wasn't a peaceful time for me.
I merely stayed silent amid internal chaos,
but that was as close as she'd ever get
and it would never be close enough for her.

I warned her about our fickle dynamic.
She wanted to see it through anyway,
believing love is about taking chances,
so the romantic in me let us play out naturally.

But the realist in me knows how this game ends.
I watched her play while I worked out of reach.
My past spun around my head, out of touch,
while she weaved potential futures in her head.

I admit that I truly enjoyed her company,
but I knew it would end soon enough.
I never told her that I loved her.
I should have.

I found a wonderful woman to take care of me,
but my stubborn heart didn't cooperate.

OUT OF HAND

I look at you, but I see her
that's not fair to you
or to me
or to her

she's in the corner of my eye
in the bottom of my heart
I can't be present with you
if I live in the past with her

she's in the back of my mind
she's in my hair and under my skin
I'm in her palm, under her thumb
so you can't touch me

I'm lost in the minutiae of regret and doubt
replaying every little detail of every argument
which helped illuminate my epiphany
        I realize you are just like her

you're infuriated by what you walked into
blaming me as if I knew you and I would meet
you're jealous of her control over me
because you want me under yours instead

I remember that I control my lock and key though
so I walked away from both of you
otherwise I'd merely move out of her hands
and right into yours

I took my heart back into my own hands

HERE'S LOOKING AT YOU

You were prepared to run just about anywhere
desperate to escape your past and present

so you grabbed my hand and lunged
but I didn't budge

because I feared your ideal future
I didn't see our potential like you did

hurt written all over your face
I never thought I'd be the author

if I could be anything –
I'd be what you need

my heart breaks knowing I can't be that man

you place yourself on standby
but it's not fair for me to ask that of you

you thought you needed me for your journey
but I assure you that I'm not necessary

we have different destinies waiting for us
so please go meet your future

SECTION 7

I MUST BE CRAZY

Give a piece of heartbreak
in exchange for a bigger piece of wisdom.

SEXY THERAPY

I've spent so much time alone
but I'm not ready to start dating yet
right now, I just want to sleep with someone
but I'm not referring to sex

I want to sleep through the night beside a gentle woman
rest my heavy mind next to a peaceful woman
to breathe deep and slow within her warm embrace
place my dizzy head on her breasts

wrap my arms around her curves
turn off the phones so we cuddle uninterrupted
we can talk about our deepest emotions
I want to shower with her and wash her hair

we could laugh or we could cry together
light candles and enjoy comfort food
set up the perfect playlist for our weekend's soundtrack
massage my shoulders and I'll rub your feet

I don't want any talk of commitment
no promises, expectations, pressure or façades
two humans connecting for peace in small moments
companionship to ward off the sadness for a while

we just need our shoulders to lean on
our ears to listen and our arms to hold
my bitterness needs a worthy opponent
we'll be sweet to each other for a little while

ONE BY ONE

Sweeping up the mess we made
s i f t i n g through our remains b i t b y b i t

cleaning up our b r o k e n p i e c e s
c r u m b b y c r u m b

mumbling thoughts of you like a madman
can't think or speak clearly like a fluency disorder

I couldn't even pronounce your name
stuttering for m – mm – mo – m o n t h s

though I'm slowly regaining control of my voice
w o r d b y w o r d

I couldn't sleep in the middle of my own bed
but I g r a d u a l l y

get more centered
i n c h b y i n c h

securing jurisdiction over my bedroom n i g h t b y n i g h t
chasing my aspirations d r e a m b y d r e a m

I've been taking ownership of my faults f l a w b y f l a w
and I'm reclaiming my lost identity p i e c e b y p i e c e

just like I write poetry l i n e b y l i n e
I put my life back together d a y b y d a y

FALLEN EMPIRE

It took me two years to finally get over you
I dreamed about us holding hands

that's when I knew I truly forgave you
I woke up that morning in a new stage of my life

we must study history if we want a better tomorrow
but I won't live in the past any longer than I already have

I know very well that you were never my enemy
we just lost ourselves in our differences and defenses

unfortunately, we overlooked our similarities
worst of all – we hurt each other in self-righteousness

I still think of you as a queen
despite our petty wars

we must remember to respect ourselves royally
and treat each other with equal class

I apologize for any of my ignoble mistakes
and you have humbly expressed your remorse as well

you're capable of rebuilding any lifestyle you want
whether you are alone or with a new partner by your side

I have no doubts of your potential
because I know your strengths

I feel no ill will toward your future gains
I believe we both came out of our wreckage as better people

AND THEN SOME

I gave you everything I had and then some.
I have nothing left at the moment.
Yes, I gained some wise love lessons,
lots of patience, understanding, and female insights.
I'm sure the next woman I love will appreciate it,
but I don't think I can give my next lover everything I gave you.

I'm afraid I may not have anything left at all
because I emptied out my heart for you.
I'm afraid my love might be in limited supply.
Your greedy heart used me up.
I swear I gave you my all, but it wasn't enough.
Or maybe I just didn't have the right stuff.

I couldn't have possibly given you anything else.
No, I wouldn't say I regret my efforts,
but I'm still angry that we didn't find forever.
I wish I spent my love on someone else,
but that someone else may not have worked out either.
So all I can do is feel proud of myself for the way I loved you.

It may not be much, but I offered my whole self to my exes,
and became a better version of myself with each new lover,
because I matured with each relationship as I aged.
So the next lover I find will meet an improved version.
This epiphany gives me a little hope for my next romance.
Praying I'll be that much of an all around better man.

I'm eager to see what skills I acquire through all of this.
So I have to sit in these feelings for just a little longer.
I must recoup, heal, learn, and grow a little more.
Hard to imagine, but I think I'll be able to love again one day,
and give a new girl everything I got,
and then some.

REFURBISHED MODELS

We're all a little used, but we got plenty of life in us
plenty of love in us, plenty of use, and plenty value

like old toys waiting for someone new to play with
hoping a bargain shopper buys us the way we are

because not everyone can afford a shiny new model
some people never inhaled the new car smell

you and I are looking for the right replacement parts
and we may be just the thing we need for each other

some people throw hearts away like they're disposable
as if they can buy a new heart at the local farmer's market

I lost a lot of women, but I kept all of their broken promises
I recycled all of their lies into my own emotional wisdom

we can repurpose pain into valuable silver linings
we can create futures that don't resemble our pasts

a few women upcycled me like an arts and crafts project
took this beaten up boy and made me a better man

and I've restored a few women after they endured hard times
so please take care of yourselves and each other

RETURN TO THE WORLD

We loved a song that encapsulated us,
but that's not our song any more.
It never belonged to us anyway
and we're no longer together
so we must return it to the world.

From our favorite songs and movies
to restaurants and vacation destinations –
none of those things ever belonged to us.
We create connections to people, places, and things
until breakups require us to unplug our connections.

I hid in a cave to lick my wounds and reorient myself
to disconnect all the attachments we shared,
and now that I've untied those knots,
that entangled us and strangled us,
I'm free and untethered from my past.

Ready to build new connections to new people and places
yet with a new profound understanding
of how we truly never own anything in this life
only our experiences – temporarily
and the world can never take those from us.

We built our own tiny universe detached from reality.
Our thoughts and emotions were severely impaired,
but I escaped our madness and found my new self.
I'm growing into my upgraded version
and my newfound sanity returns me to the world.

SUITED

You loved other bearded men
before you snuggled in my stubble
before you slept on my chest
so I believe you will love another guy after me

liars and abusers mistreated you
but you still found a way to trust me,
so I assume you'll get over our breakup
and find another man soon enough

I hope you learned from our time together
and find someone whose better suited for you,
I know I discovered a lot about myself
and I hope I find someone well suited for me

I lived within the curves of other women
before I moved into yours
before I found a home in your aura
so I think I can love another soul after you

far from perfect, but I'm actively working on myself
I thank you for our time together
I doubt the world possesses a girl tailored for me,
but I'll continue to search for my great match

QUIET IN THE END   (for Stephanie)

Heaven bleeds into earth
smooth as the passage of time
I'm glad our final moments were quiet and sweet

the world's clock stood still for us briefly
when we held each other naked in bed
hiding from the deafening city

mad at this entire world
because nobody ever cried for us
runaways abandoned under postpartum

past traumas sewn to us like shadows
but you and I stuck together
I'm sorry for what I did and what I didn't do

it was difficult to recall a quiet memory
but I found one hiding behind the remorse in my heart
under those 911 calls and between our hospital visits

trying my hardest to move on and do better
I've been praying ever since you left
for the white yonder to overlook our wrongs

we were merely kids living at full volume
I thank God we had a few quiet moments in the end
I hope you rest in peace like that again

I SAID YOUR NAME ALOUD   (for Stephanie)

Memories flood my conscious
run amok around my brain
chills shoot through my nerves

so many years have passed
that our story is hard to believe
trauma old enough to feel like a bad dream
like we never shared our lives together

but you certainly lived
my aging tears are still very much alive
that stabbing pain in my heart is immortal

our screams still echo through time
my deepest fears continue to shake me
and survivor's guilt still weighs heavy
operating and idling, but my heart is still not still

all these years after your passing
my tears still drip onto every line
flooding every stanza written for you

remorse zigzags through my mind
like a pen crossing out mistakes on paper
unable to apologize or make things right
unable to show you all my growth thus far

envisioning your face still brings me joy
your smile carves a smirk on my face
your laugh slices a sliver of hope in my heart

I send my deepest love to you
I pray that you're better now and in a safe place
Stephanie – maybe you hear me
when I say your name aloud

VANISHING (for Stephanie)

Memories of you
enveloped me once like skin
scars and beauty marks
my mind is shedding of you

Memories of you
can't find the time to visit
like a protégé who surpassed a mentor
my brain could be failing me or protecting me

Memories of you
don't come around as often
but at least I have some nightmares
the pain is better than nothing at all

Memories of you
elude me as if they detest me
I promise you this isn't on purpose
I'm sorry if you feel forgotten

Memories of you
robbed from me as time steals so many details
each passing day pickpockets a remnant of you
I'm guilty of being human amid fleeting time

Memories of you
disappear without a trace
it's getting harder to remember you
I hate how you're vanishing

KNEE-JERK

I can't stop talking to you in my head
even though I haven't seen you in a year,
talking to the walls and an empty chair

we were the first ones we called with news
the last voice, vision, and kiss at night,
we were each other's habits

you hated how I could finish your sentences,
I tickled your kneecaps and you'd call me a jerk,
we were each other's knee-jerk reactions,

we had a rhythm, a system, a reflex memory
I did A and you did B like clockwork,
but we also knew how to push each other's buttons

we subconsciously grow accustomed to our dailies,
but my memories of distinct trivialities are fading
I'm sure they'll disappear completely sooner or later

just like it took time to stop missing you
I have no desire to speak with you again,
but I still have conversations with you in my head

I want to say certain comments to make people laugh,
but then I realize you're the only person
who would understand our inside joke

any kind of auto response is difficult to retrain
I must replace old reflexes with healthier reactions
I need new behaviors to erase old habits

I need someone new to talk to

APPREHENSION

Apprehensive girls and petrified boys
must unlearn toxic behaviors taught to us.
We must recognize the red flags in others
and avoid making the same mistakes twice.

Try your best to make appropriate changes.
You're strong enough to break habits.
Forgive past indiscretions and let go of regrets.
We're all capable of this emotional growth.

Keep an eye out for other people growing spiritually –
those are the mindful people you want around you.
It's a learning process like anything else.
We are all a work-in-progress.

From divorce and restraining orders
to abuse and failure to communicate,
but remember the protective walls we build
can also lock out the good with the bad.

I won't claim I'll never hurt you,
that's a fool's promise,
but I swear to never harm you on purpose.
And that's all I ask of you in return.

Marrow soaked in trauma,
heart marinated in fear,
but I'm made with love, warmth, and passion,
so I want to get back out there,

but I'm still full of apprehension

MINEFIELDS AND EGGSHELLS

I tiptoed through her internal wars
because she lived in a minefield,
you walked on eggshells through his life
because he broke everything around you

I ran away from her as fast as I could
praying I didn't step on any explosives,
and the police removed him from your life
only time will remove him from your mind

hearts often take their sweet time
regardless of our plans or preferred pace
you and I both had our share of battles
so we understand each other in a way most people can't

we respect each other's journeys and feel comfortable together
our hearts beat faster upon meeting, but we both remain timid
I'm excited for the new spark flickering between us
yet afraid of the wick connecting us that may detonate

equally unsure of the force pulling us forward
as we are angry at our trauma dragging us backward,
you and I don't believe we would treat one another poorly,
but we might break if we're wrong again

maybe I present calmly, but I'm just as afraid as you are
though I still take your hand and take the first step
hoping you follow my lead and walk beside me
despite our deep fears of minefields and eggshells

I MUST BE CRAZY

Unhealthy relationships can destroy us
yet isolation can make a person go stir-crazy.
So we need to find balance
and the right person can foster our serenity.

I thought I knew what I wanted when I was young,
but nothing happened the way I wanted it to.
So now I reevaluate what I need in a relationship
because it's time I begin dating again.

Yeah, I've been tortured in the past,
but not everyone is an abuser.
Whether you call it love or psychopathy –
so many hearts around the world keep believing.

I suppose I've healed from my heartbreak,
but won't truly know until I pressure test with someone.
And I just met an incredible woman
so I thank her for reintroducing me to eagerness.

Plato explained how love is a serious mental disease.
Maybe you'll go crazy for me and I'll get silly for you,
but maybe we're mature enough to stay levelheaded
and maybe we can be each other's peace.

Potential love is worth the risk
so I collect my lessons and gather my bravery.
I hope for the best and prepare for the worst.
I'm about to take another shot at this thing called *love*.

I must be crazy

FRANCO'S MESSAGE

My relationships challenged everything I knew, which made me feel crazy, but I've also encountered the healing power of love. I try to let go of the pain while still holding the lessons. *Love is a Mental Illness* may be educational in some way, but it's primarily art to entertain. This poetry collection is not any kind of advice.

Too many people harm themselves when their heart hurts. I grew up with many friends who self-harmed and attempted suicide. Some friends did commit suicide. And I also harmed myself as a child.

This is partly why I focus on strengthening my mental health and one of the many reasons why I became a licensed social worker. I've counseled adolescents struggling with mental health issues and suicidal ideation. Education and exposure desensitize us, but these situations don't become any easier to cope with.

We invest a significant amount of energy and time into our relationships. They become our whole world and other people become less important. Humans rely on security and physical contact, and these emotional bonds become essential to our self-identity. So we struggle with letting go when relationships end.

People try to fill this void. Unfortunately, many of us lack positive outlets and healthy coping skills. It's easy to resort to self-medicating and other risky behaviors. I know the pain can seem unbearable, but I promise you that the hurt will heal. You have so much to offer this world and so much to look forward to in life.

I suggest you speak with friends and family if you're struggling with heartache. And I strongly encourage you to speak with an experienced mental health professional. This world has people with big hearts, just like you. You don't have to go through hard times alone. You are not alone. Help is only a phone call away.

My heart goes out to you all.

- Franco

HELP IS ONLY A PHONE CALL AWAY

NATIONAL DOMESTIC VIOLENCE HOTLINE (U.S.A.)
CALL: 1.800.799.7233
You can text "START" to 88788
Visit their website @ TheHotline.org

NATIONAL SEXUAL ASSAULT HOTLINE (U.S.A.)
CALL: 1.800.656.4673
You can also chat with them on their website @ Rainn.org

CRISIS TEXT LINE:
You can text "HOME" to 741741 (U.S.A.)
You can text "HOME" to 85258 (United Kingdom)
You can text "HOME" to 686868 (Canada)

SUICIDE AND CRISIS LIFELINE (U.S.A.)
CALL: 988

THANK YOU

If you enjoyed reading *Love Is a Mental Illness*, please leave a review or choose a star rating. Reviews are crucial for authors.

Thank you for spending time with my work.
I'm truly grateful.

Love and literature
– Franco

Sign-up to receive new book alerts @ FrancoCardiello.com

Interact with me on Instagram @ FrancoCardiello

ABOUT THE AUTHOR

Franco Cardiello is a novelist and poet from New York. After living in the juvenile justice system, he earned his master's in clinical social work from Fordham University. He became a licensed counselor to provide therapy and creative writing to teenagers in residential facilities. His art and his counseling often overlap. Art is one aspect of his therapeutic approach, while psychology plays a major influence on his artwork. Much of his writing explores trauma, societal taboos, love, and family. Franco hopes his work can bring some solace to a distressed world.

Made in the USA
Coppell, TX
26 September 2023